# APOSTOLIC TEAM MINISTRY

## Releasing Heaven's Provision on Earth

## Scott Wallis

Lighthouse Publications

© 2003 by Scott Wallis

**Apostolic Team Ministry**
by Scott Wallis

Printed in the United States of America
ISBN 0-9642211-2-8

Unless otherwise indicated, Bible quotations are taken from the King James Version.

Publisher
Lighthouse Publications
2028 Larkin Avenue
Elgin, IL 60123
(847) 468-1457
www.LightTheNations.com

Author
Scott Wallis
www.ScottWallis.org

Cover Design
Scott Wallis & Associates
2028 Larkin Avenue
Elgin, IL 60123
(847) 468-1457

# Foreword

by Bob & Kim Sperlazzo

The office of the apostle is well-established in the Bible – it's a foundation in the New Testament (Eph. 2:20; 1 Cor. 12:28). And yet, it is not operational in most of the Church today. Paul wrote in Ephesians 4 about the five foundational offices, the Gifts of Christ to the Church, as being *"apostles, ...prophets, ...evangelists, ...pastors and teachers..."* (v. 11). And, for what purpose did He give these offices?

*"...For the perfecting of the saints, for the work of the ministry, for the edifying of the body of Christ: till we all come in the unity of the faith, and of the knowledge of the Son of God, unto a perfect man, unto the measure of the stature of the fulness of Christ: that we henceforth be no more children, tossed to and fro, and carried about with every wind of doctrine, by the sleight of men, and cunning craftiness, whereby they lie in wait to deceive"* (v. 12-15).

The fact is that, for the above passage to be fulfilled, ALL of the "five-fold ministry" offices are of absolute necessity. The Church today desperately needs a clearer understanding of how these five offices function together.

While the offices and ministries of the pastor, teacher and evangelist have been embraced and supported for decades, the offices of the apostle and prophet have been held at arm's length and denied their proper place in the modern-day Church. Those of God's servants who respond to pastoral, teaching and evangelistic calls in their lives are affirmed and celebrated. At the same time, those who dare to respond to a calling to the apostolic or prophetic ministries are treated with suspicion or held up to scrutinizing criticism and impossibly high and exacting standards. How can we not take the whole counsel of the Word of God, picking words out of verses and discarding them as irrelevant?

Of course, the most well known of the apostles are the original twelve, along with Paul. But, others are also named as apostles throughout the New Testament, including Matthias, who replaced Judas (Acts 1:26), Barnabas, who traveled with Paul (Acts 14:4), Andronicus and Junia (Rom. 16:7), and others. Each of these was chosen much later, which shows God's establishing precedence for the Church, even unto these present days, as many present-day apostles have demonstrated.

We Believers who have been raised and grounded on the Word of God cannot afford to dissect that very Word by removing or disregarding the parts we don't want to believe. Sadly, today, many who say they are Believers selectively choose passages from the Word of God like a menu. But, let us not be as those who would add to or take away from the eternal Word of God (Rev. 22:18-19)!

The fact is that no one has a complete understanding of ALL the truth, not even seasoned church leadership. We all have "blind spots," and we need one another to help us see what we ourselves cannot, in order to discover the whole truth in the Word of God. God doesn't subscribe to our denominational doctrines and creeds – He desires us to accept HIS Word as truth, and by that truth, to measure all of our doctrines and traditions.

Our revelation and understanding of God's truth may increase, but God's Word remains forever true. It extends to us the simple, real life power of God working in and through our lives for His glory. To deny the truths in His Word leaves us powerless – an empty, apostate shell that merely resembles His Body, the Church. As Paul rightly predicted, *"in the last days...having a form of godliness, but denying the power thereof"* (2 Tim. 3:1-5).

Many of our old methods and traditions are ineffective. The new wine that God would give us cannot be contained within our old wineskins (Mk. 2:22). We must be willing to be sifted and measured against the Word to search our hearts and purify our motives, along with the outworking of our ways in our lives and ministries – both personal and corporate.

This book contains many foundational truths and clear understandings of God's own heart and ways. *"For My thoughts are not your thoughts, neither are your ways My ways,' saith the LORD. 'For as the heavens are higher than the earth, so are My ways higher than your ways, and My thoughts than your thoughts. '"* (Is. 55:8-9).

Understanding apostolic team ministry is one important key to opening up our ability to more fully cooperate with God in releasing His bountiful blessings upon the earth. To grasp these truths will bring increase in our effectiveness, fulfilling our destinies as individuals as well as churches or ministries.

The Church can no longer afford the "Business as Usual" mindset, because Jesus is returning for a *"glorious Church, not having spot, or wrinkle, or any such thing; but that it should be holy and without blemish"* (Eph. 5:27). The old performance and programs must make way for the fresh move of God, if we are to discover and partake of the new wine – His long-awaited outpouring upon this generation and those yet to come.

*Bob & Kim Sperlazzo are ordained in local church eldership and a "five-fold" ministry capacity. For 40 years, Bob & Kim have been involved with prophetic, teaching, worship and evangelistic ministry with an emphasis on reaching, raising up and releasing this generation of youth. Together, they minister through **3-D Generations**, a ministry to those of all ages who are "Distressed, and in Debt, and Discontented" (1 Sam. 22:2), just as those who later became the "Mighty Men of David." Bob is also the editor of **Informed Christian Digest**, a national newsletter by email. Together, they live in the Chicago area with their five children.*

• Apostolic Team Ministry •

# Contents

Foreword ............................................................... v

Introduction ........................................................... 1

Chapter One
Apostolic Teams: Desperately Needed Now ............ 19

Chapter Two
Apostolic Teams Defined, and How They Work ....... 43

Chapter Three
Agreement in Prayer: A Team's Source of Power ..... 65

Chapter Four
Receiving Revelation of Apostolic Team Ministry ...... 83

Chapter Five
Transferring the World's Wealth to the Church ........ 95

# Introduction

The message contained in this book began as a simple desire within my heart and the heart of another man to get together and pray. When we originally started our times of prayer, we had no idea how important these would become to both of us. There was something wonderful that started happening as God began answering our prayers. All of a sudden, we were in the midst of promotion. I was being promoted in the spiritual realm through ministry, and this other man was being promoted in the natural realm through business.

Through this, God started revealing to me the power of effective prayer. I started understanding what James meant when he said, *"Confess your faults one to another, and pray one for another, that ye may be healed"* (Jas. 5:16). This is what we did. We confessed our needs to each other and prayed over these personal needs, wants and desires. As a result, the blessing of God came upon both of our lives. It has come to such a place that neither of us wants to miss these times of prayer.

Because of the level of blessing we were experiencing, I began to open this meeting up to others. Gradually over time, people started coming.

Although the attendance size was never very large, we did have some powerful times of prayer. Yet, it was evident to both me and this other man that there was something missing – an ingredient that we previously had was gone.

Suddenly, we started experiencing problems with lack. Our finances were suffering, whereas before, there had been plenty. Our relationships experienced different misunderstandings, whereas before, there were clear lines of communication. Even our spiritual lives were diminished – we weren't hearing as clearly from heaven as we had been. As a result, I began seeking God for answers to where we had missed Him. Out of this time of seeking has come the message revealed in this book on apostolic team ministry.

## Plugging into Apostolic Power

What neither I nor this other man realized is that we, through our times of prayer, were tapping into a power that we didn't know was available the power of apostolic team ministry. We had unlocked a key that we were using to advance the kingdom of God through our lives that we didn't even know was available. God, through our desire to follow Him, had placed us upon a path of blessing in spite of our own ignorance regarding how His Kingdom works.

God used our natural needs, wants and desires to place within us an understanding that heretofore has not yet been understood by the Body of Christ: apostolic team ministry. We, through our times of prayer, had become an apostolic team, even though we didn't realize it at the time. God used us in a number of ways, including starting a radio ministry overseas, a church in the States and implementing an innovative marketing plan within business. We were prospering as two people who had a genuine desire to serve God.

God was honoring us by answering our prayers. We were receiving significant answers to prayer that was literally propelling us forward into a place of promotion, naturally and spiritually. We had unlocked the secret of not only answered prayer, but also bringing heaven upon earth. We were experiencing a little taste of heaven, and it was great!

## Finding Where We Missed God

It was so great that, when we lost it, we were willing to do anything to get it back. We wanted to have what we had lost, and so we needed to find out from God what was wrong with us and why things had changed in the way we were receiving answers from Him. We retraced our steps, seeing where we had gone and what we had changed.

This is the point that most people miss: we had changed something that we were doing, and as a result, it had separated us from the answers God wanted to give. We needed to change; otherwise, what had been happening in our lives would not continue. So, this is what we did: we started changing.

Through the process of elimination, we realized that by inviting other people to our prayer meeting, we were in effect watering down the power of our prayers. Our prayers were not being answered because there was not total agreement as there had been previously. We had opened the door to others, but inadvertently closed the door to God. We were hindering God from answering our prayers, because we weren't doing things His way as revealed in His Word.

Immediately upon changing this one thing, God began to reopen doors to us. This book is a product of that change. If we had not been willing to change, it is highly unlikely that things would have changed for me or the other man. We would still be in a tough spot, because we were violating a principle revealed in God's Word that we had been using to obtain His blessing. We had obtained God's blessing, because we were walking in accordance with His Word. When we stopped walking in accordance with His Word, we lost His blessing. God's blessing always comes according to His Word.

## Understanding God's Ways

If you are like me, you may ask yourself the question: How could inviting other people to a prayer meeting cause God to remove His blessing? The answer, although sound scripturally, may be tough for some to swallow, because it violates what they have previously been taught about the way God works. And, God doesn't do what we think He should, but rather what He has already said He would do according to His Word.

The Word of God is the basis for all that we do in the Church. When we do something in the Church, it should be because there is a revelation of it in God's Word. Without this foundation for what we are doing, we will inevitably give in to the winds and the waves that surround us in this world. As Paul said, *"other foundation can no man lay than that is laid...*" (1 Cor. 3:11). God's Word is the only foundation that cannot be shaken by anything in or out of this world.

Jesus, God's Living Word, is the way that we are called to build the Kingdom of God. It is by understanding Him and the way that He did things that we are able to follow in His footsteps. Unless we know how Christ walked, how can we walk with Him? This is the only way that we will do what Jesus did, walk as Jesus walked and live like He lived. Our calling is to live and move and have our being in Him. This is the essence of genuine apostolic ministry.

## Apostles: The Man and Ministry

Apostolic ministry is not just a title that we possess, but also a lifestyle that we live. We live as He lived, because we have learned from Him how to walk as He walked and do what He did. This is why we can do His works and be sent by Him to various people groups around the world. The signs of an apostle are wrought to confirm the character of the man as well as the calling of the ministry.

The Church has tried to remove the man from the ministry, but I am here to tell you that it just can't be done. The man and the ministry are one

8

even as the Father and the Son are one. We cannot be apostles on Sunday and devils on Monday. Apostle are apostles because they have passed the tests presented to them by the Father and walked through the refining fires of His presence to become a vessel that can be used to contain His glory. This is genuine apostolic ministry.

I do not believe that a man or woman who has not been through tests, trials and tribulations is a commissioned representative of Christ on earth as an apostle. They may function in one of the other ministry gifts and be called as an apostle, but they are not apostles yet, because they have not gone through the refining fires of God. Each ministry gift has its own unique levels of requirements, which must be met by us before we can begin walking in it.

## Relationship is the Key

Although I do not believe that apostles are in hierarchical ascension over other ministry gifts, their relationship to Christ is different than the other ministry gifts and as such they do have a greater authority from Him. It is this authority from God that is the foundation of what they do. Without this authority, individuals cannot be genuine apostles of Christ.

The authority about which I am speaking is not positional in their relationship to man, but relational in their relationship with God. Apostles have greater authority from God, because they have been through more with Him, and as such, have paid the price necessary to be trusted by Him with a different level of authority. This is the heart of the issue over who is the greatest in the kingdom of God – he/she that has learned how to become a servant to God and His purposes in the earth. A true apostle becomes a bond slave to the purposes of Christ and the Church in the earth.

Just because we think that we are servants to Christ doesn't mean that we are walking as servants. A servant is one who has learned how to walk with His master and not be offended by Him or others. As long as we hold to our petty strivings for power, prestige and position, we cannot be the servants of Christ. Those who long to be well known by men are putting themselves in a position that will steal from their calling in Christ.

## Doing What Jesus is Doing

Christ did not call us to be well known or unknown, but rather, to do what we see Him doing. This is the crux of true ministry – doing what we see Jesus doing in the same way He did what He saw His Father doing. As such, there are many who think that because they are well known and heard by many that they have greater authority with God and man. Others think that because they are unknown, what they are doing is irrelevant or unimportant. These are both lies from the pit of hell that have caused many to fall into error.

Christ's Kingdom is not entrepreneurial in nature. Christ calls whom He wills to do His work as He wills. The way this happens is through the communication of His blessing. Unfortunately, many people have supported works, for years, which have not blessed them. Supporting ministries that do not release God's blessing into our lives is unscriptural. We must understand that there is a tangible blessing released to us as we financially support anointed churches and ministries. This is why many tithe and give offerings, yet are never blessed; they haven't given to those men or women who have the ability to communicate their blessing to us.

This is how men and women commissioned by Christ as apostles will establish apostolic team ministry through the communication of the blessing of God. Understand this, dear saints of God: If we don't support apostolic ministries, not only will *we* suffer, but also the ministry itself will suffer. This is why it is so important that we support with our finances those apostolic ministries that have blessed us.

## Apostolic Teams Bring Real Unity

Apostolic team ministry is different from other ministry being offered today, in that, it may not come from what we would call the local church. This term, although good for classifying churches, is not Biblical in nature. Even the term "local church" is not scriptural. Churches in the New Testament were not categorized by their doctrine or denomination, but rather by their city.

The Church in the New Testament consisted of citywide churches that were made up of local men with five-fold ministry callings who were called elders. It was these men who governed the citywide church. The Church itself was never meant to be divided; it became divided through heresy and carnality. The Church today needs to hear what Paul said to the church in Corinth: *"For ye are yet carnal: for whereas there is among you envying and strife and divisions, are ye not carnal, and walk as men?"* (1 Cor. 3:3).

To most of us this may sound like a low blow, but it is the truth. In spite of all our great advances, the Church today is still carnal because we lack unity in the Body of Christ. This is why apostolic team ministry is so important, for it will help restore unity to the Body of Christ in practical ways through the release of the tangible blessing of God.

So then, apostolic team ministry is not just a ministry of the word, but of the power, presence, provision and protection of Christ through the release of the tangible blessing of God. It is this blessing that we so desperately need and can only be gained through apostolic team ministry. The commanded blessing of God is only available through the corporate unity of the Church, which can only happen through the spiritual dynamic of apostolic team ministry.

## Becoming an Apostolic Church

Apostolic team ministry comes through the commission of Christ. It is the pattern upon which all the churches in the New Testament were founded. Every church in the New Testament was connected in some way to an apostle. Apostles were accessible and available to city churches for the purpose of establishing Christ's kingdom. Often

13

these apostolic teams would stay in a city for months, even years, for the purpose of building the Church in that city.

Apostles and apostolic teams were willing to sacrifice their time and energy for the sake of building the kingdom of God in a particular territory. As such, the churches within those territories were called to support these men and women. When they did this, all was well. When they didn't do this, they lost the blessing of God, and the apostles or apostolic team would shake the dust off their feet and move to the next city. And believe me, when this happened, that community felt the shockwaves of it.

The Early Church had a sense of community that we don't have today. We have lost what this sense of community brought – genuine fellowship. The reason we have so little true fellowship around Christ in the Church is that we have not known what the Church is or is called to become.

The Church is called to become something greater than just a teaching, training, equipping and empowering invading army. We are also called to something greater than a compassionate, loving, giving, serving, healing, delivering and evangelistic Body of Believers. We are called to become the family of God, and this can only happen in the context of real people who love Christ and each other. This is why we need real relationships of love in the context of a community of Believers who are committed to one another through covenant.

As we move forward in this book, I am going to be sharing more about the exact nature of apostolic team ministry. The next chapter will describe in great detail what apostolic team ministry is, and why it is important to the Church. Suffice it to say that, unless this ministry is restored to the Church, we will not be able to enter into the blessing that God wants to bring into our lives, and the world-wide Church will be limited in it's effectiveness.

I believe that it is God's desire to birth this kind of ministry in the earth at this time, because it has the potential to bring His blessing in greater ways than we have ever seen before. Because of this, I want to ask you to consider what I say, and may the Lord give you understanding of all these things.

• Apostolic Team Ministry •

# Chapter One

• Apostolic Team Ministry •

# Apostolic Teams: Desperately Needed Now

C hrist, when He ascended on high and gave gifts to men, gave some to be apostles (Eph. 4:10-11). Jesus has called certain men or women to carry the call of apostleship. This calling is not given to every member of the Body of Christ (1 Cor. 12:29). As such they are unique to the Body of Christ. Apostles are not only distinct in their function, but also unique in their calling.

When Christ called some to be apostles, He gave them something specific that He called them to do. An apostle without a mission or mandate is not an apostle. Apostles by function are men or women who know what Christ has called them to do, beyond a shadow of doubt. They know His will for their lives, and as such, are striving to fulfill that will.

The will of God is not stepped into easily. Scripture declares: *"...the kingdom of heaven suffereth violence, and the violent take it by force"* (Matt. 11:12). And, according to Paul, *"We have this treasure in earthen vessels, that the excellency of the power may be of God, and not of us"* (2 Cor. 4:7). God has placed within apostles the ability and authority to bring His kingdom on earth as it is in heaven. This is what apostles seek to do through their lives and ministries.

## A Servant for Jesus' Sake

Genuine apostles are not looking to promote themselves. No, they are looking to change things that are out of alignment in the Church or world system on earth to match the pattern that is revealed in heaven. God has placed within them the vision of the way things should or could be. Apostles are not capitalists or communists, but Christians with a desire to bring the kingdom of Christ on earth as it is in heaven.

The Church was never called to be a democracy. We have reduced the government of God, which is theocratic in nature, into the poll of public opinion. If one member is not satisfied with their place or position in Christ, all they need to do is market themselves to the masses and they will have a ministry. Is this not the way things are done in our day?

We have so little discernment that we can barely tell when Christ is with us. We do not know what is from God, because for most of us, we have not been with Him. Paul bade the Corinthian believers with this comment: *"Examine yourselves, whether ye be in the faith"* (2 Cor. 13:5). We would do well if we did the same.

We have lost so much over the course of time, that we can barely see beyond the shadows that surround us. The darkness has seemed to overwhelm the Church and world. We have more hype with less hope that we have ever had before. This is why we need to recover the role that genuine apostles play in the Church – we desperately need them!

21

## Receiving the Apostolic Mission

Apostles are vital to the growth of the Church, not just numerically, but spiritually. Genuine apostles are men or women who know how to disciple new Believers to become God fearing leaders. Apostles have what it takes to impart the nature of Christ to those they meet in such a way that they understand the nature of the gospel of Christ.

The gospel of Christ is not in word only, but in power and assurance. It is this inward witness and outward display that makes manifest the apostolic ministry in the lives of those who have it. We cannot miss an apostle, but we may ignore them because they do not fit our image of what an apostle should be. This is why we need to take to heart the counsel of Scripture, which is: *"Be not forgetful to entertain strangers: for thereby some have entertained angels unawares"* (Heb. 13:2).

Jesus said, *"He that receiveth whomsoever I send receiveth Me; and he that receiveth Me receiveth him that sent Me"* (Jn. 13:20). When we do not receive those who are called as apostles, we are equally rejecting the One they represent. This is why it is so important for us to understand that apostles, although men, contain a ministry that is greater than themselves.

## What is an Apostle?

An apostle is nothing more than a servant of Christ, anointed by Him for a specific purpose that requires an extraordinary degree of discipline and fortitude to complete. Because of this, they are given special gifts abilities and anointings to accomplish this work. This is what sets them apart from other ministry gifts.

Apostles have a mission that they themselves cannot complete, an adversary they cannot avoid, and are sent to a people who may reject, persecute or kill them. Talk about impossible mission – this is what apostles have been given by Christ. How would you like this kind of ministry? I think that few of us in our right minds would willingly choose this type of ministry.

Apostles are given greater authority and greater responsibility, because they themselves have paid the price to follow God. Christ can trust them with more because they have been through more for the purpose of refining their hearts. They are surrounded by the fire of God, and are often in the midst of that same fire themselves for the purpose of their own purification.

The calling of an apostle is not to preach himself, but rather Christ Jesus the Lord, and to be himself a servant for Jesus' sake. The primary message of an apostle is Jesus Christ, and Him crucified (1 Cor. 2:2). They preach Christ because they long to see Christ. Christ is their all-in-all, and because of this, they are willing to count anything else as dung to gain the matchless treasures of the risen Christ.

Apostles will not settle for second best. They will not roll over and play dead. If you knock an apostle down, he will get right back up. This is the persistence and longsuffering that it takes to be an apostle. Their lives are known by the level of perseverance they possess in pursuing the cause of Christ. This is what makes an apostle different from all the other ministry gifts.

Because of the level of opposition that an apostle will encounter on their way to fulfilling the cause for which Christ has called them, they have a special measure of faith. This measure of faith is resident within them for the purpose of carrying them to their destination. The operation of this apostolic faith is very similar to that of the gift of faith, in that, it is a supernatural faith from Christ, given for the purpose of building the kingdom of Christ.

Why have I spent so much time talking about apostles? Because, although there are books available on apostles, they do not carry the crux of what an apostle will face in their ministry. Apostles are not primarily governmental figures in the Church, but the foundation of the Church (Eph. 2:20). This means that there is a greater calling and responsibility placed upon apostles than we have even realized.

Apostles are essential members of the Body of Christ. In the same way that a human body will die without a beating heart, the Church will abide in a place of death apart from the ministry of apostles. This is why we need to hear the word of the Lord to the Church in this generation, which is, *"Awake thou that sleepest and arise from the dead, and Christ shall give thee light"* (Eph. 5:14).

## Apostles in the Early Church

When we take a look at apostolic ministry in the Early Church, there seems to be a common pattern of apostles working in teams. These apostolic teams were commonly made up of two and at most three individuals who were anointed by Christ to stand in the office of apostle. These men or women were joined together by the Holy Spirit in agreement to do the work of Christ.

The first time that we see apostolic teams in operation is when Jesus, while on earth, sent forth the twelve apostles two-by-two. When He did this, He was leaving us a pattern for how apostolic ministry should function in teams of two. Jesus didn't just send them out two-by-two to keep each other company. No He did this to reveal the will of the Father as it is in heaven.

Christ, when He sent the twelve apostles forth, gave them this commandment, *"And as ye go, preach, saying, 'The kingdom of heaven is at hand.' Heal the sick, cleanse the lepers, raise the dead, cast out devils: freely ye have received, freely give"* (Matt. 10:7-8). And the Scripture says that Jesus *"gave them power against unclean spirits, to cast them out, and to heal all manner of sickness and all manner of disease"* (Matt. 10:1).

Jesus did the same thing when He sent forth the seventy disciples. He sent them forth two-by-two. Notice that Jesus didn't just tell them to go; He sent them forth. This is the core of apostolic team ministry – being sent forth by Christ to do a specific work for Him. The Scripture says that they returned saying, *"Lord even the devils are subject unto us through Thy Name"* (Lk. 10:17).

In both of these cases, Jesus sent forth apostles and apostolic teams two-by-two. If we go throughout the Book of Acts, we will see the same pattern. One of the main apostolic teams that we see in the Book of Acts is Peter and John. Notice that when they were working together, great things happened – people were saved, healed and delivered.

This same pattern can be found in the sending forth of Paul and Barnabus. The Holy Spirit sent them forth from Antioch as an apostolic team. Scripture says that the Holy Spirit said, *"Separate me Barnabas and Saul (Paul) for the work whereunto I have called them"* (Acts 13:2). God, by His Spirit, joined them together for the purpose of bringing His kingdom on earth as it is in heaven, and great things happened through their ministries.

When Paul and Barnabus split up, the first thing that they did was to choose another partner to go with them. The Scripture says *"...and so Barnabas took Mark, and sailed unto Cyprus; and Paul chose Silas, and departed, being recommended by the brethren unto the grace of God"* (Acts 15:39b-40).

27

Do you see how they believed that it was important for them to work in apostolic teams?

## The Need for Apostolic Teams Today

If this was the case then, how much more is this the case now? Apostolic teams are still the primary way that Christ sends forth His apostles. Apostles were never meant to work alone in ministry. They are meant to have specific apostolic team partners who will help carry the burden and load of the ministry. This is the essence of apostolic team ministry: *"Bear ye one another's burdens, and so fulfil the law of Christ"* (Gal. 6:2).

We as apostles are called to work with one another for the purpose of building the kingdom of God. God anoints apostolic teams to do different things. Some apostolic teams may be anointed for the purpose of prayer, as Peter and John were. Others may be missionary teams sent forth to reach unreached people groups, as were Barnabus and Paul. When Jesus raises up an apostolic team, there is always a specific team function and blessing brought by that team.

What gives apostolic teams their strength? I believe that apostolic teams receive a greater measure of grace from Christ, because they have a level of agreement with each other in Him. They have learned how to work with each other to see God's will done not only in their lives, but in the lives of those around them. Hence, apostolic teams function on a higher plane of ministry than other ministries can alone.

Do you remember when Jesus said, *"if two of you shall agree on earth as touching any thing that they shall ask, it shall be done for them of my Father which is in heaven"* (Matt. 18:19)? Notice Jesus specifically said "two," not "three, four or five." I think that sometimes we have inadvertently added to what Christ said by not fully understanding what He actually was saying.

Prior to my receiving this revelation about apostolic teams, I had heard this Scripture many times, but never related it to the fact that Jesus sent out His apostles and disciples two-by-two. It wasn't until one morning when the Holy Spirit awakened me with this Scripture in my heart, and the revelation of how these Scriptures were related to it, that I began to understand the importance of apostolic team ministry. Apostles usually work in apostolic teams of two; this is where they gain the greatest effectiveness.

Truly, the Word says one can put a thousand to flight, and two ten thousand (Deut. 32:30), but the Scripture never does say that three can put one hundred thousand to flight or four a million. I think that we have inferred things from Scripture that are not revealed in Scripture. I am not saying that there is not a greater effectiveness when more than two are in agreement, for the Scriptures reveal the power available when the Body of Christ is together in unity. What I am talking about, though, is that Christ has called apostolic teams to bring forth this unity into the Body of Christ.

How can the Body of Christ be joined together in unity if we cannot see two apostles come together in unity as an apostolic team? This, I believe, is the breeding ground for genuine unity in the Body of Christ. We need apostles to come together as apostolic teams to establish the work of Christ through apostolic team ministry. It is only when this happens that we will see Christ's kingdom come and His will done on earth as it is in heaven.

## Understanding the Battle

God's greatest desire is for His will to be done in earth as it is in heaven. The will of God is so complete and full that nothing in this world can compare to it. We are not wrestling with God to see His will done; we are wrestling with principalities, powers, rulers and wicked spirits. The devil is the one seeking to stop God's will from being done in our lives – he is our adversary.

God allows the enemy to fight us so that we can gain the victory over him. This brings the greatest glory to God. When we defeat the enemy in our lives, we are bringing great glory to our Father in heaven. This is why spiritual warfare is such an important part of the spiritual life of a believer. It is through our warfare against the adversary that we bring glory to God.

The battle between God and Satan has already been fought and won. Jesus, through his death upon the cross, defeated Satan and all of his hosts once and for all time. The Scriptures declare that He *"spoiled principalities and powers,"* making *"a show of them openly, triumphing over them in it"* (Col. 2:15). Jesus defeated the devil, and yet every day, we can see that there is still a battle raging in the earth. The question is: How can this be, since the devil was forever defeated at the cross? I believe that the answer to this question lies in the fact that the battle now raging is not between God and Satan, but between Satan and the Church.

31

The Church has, through her allegiance to Christ, become the greatest threat the devil has ever known. Through His death at the cross, Jesus gave birth to a new man called the Church. This new man is called to possess what Adam through transgression lost – the earth. This can only happen as we enforce the victory that Christ won at the cross. Through our relationship with Christ, we have been given the power and authority to do exactly this. This is the great battle raging in the earth, and it is between the devil and the Church.

The Church is largely unaware of this battle. Somehow, we have thought that God's will would be done in our lives through a supernatural spiritual osmosis – that God, apart from us, would cause His will to be done in our lives. This fallacy has pervaded the Church for centuries, and has created, as it were, a fatalistic "que sera sera" attitude in the Church, i.e., "whatever will be will be." This is one of the greatest lies to blind the Church to the true nature of her warfare, and as a result, the enemy has been able to gain the upper hand on us.

If you are wondering why things are the way they are in the earth today, all you have to do is look at what is happening in the Church. Unless we realize that we have a part to play in the eternal purposes of God and begin seeing ourselves through the light of God's Word, we will never become all that God intended us to be. And we know that God will never allow this to happen.

God has invested a great deal in the Church. He bought and birthed it through the blood of His Son. How long do you think God will allow a weak-willed, worldly-minded Church to be at the forefront of what He is doing? Will not God begin fighting against this type of Church and give birth to another type of Church purified through the refining fires of His presence? I think that it is time that we evaluate ourselves to see if we are in the faith.

God does not care if we are Evangelical, Catholic, Baptist, Methodist or any host of denominations. What He does care about is the truth of Christ being promoted through the Church. The Church according to Scripture is called to be *"the pillar and ground of the truth"* in the earth (1 Tim. 3:15). The truth in Christ is our greatest weapon in our fight to regain what the devil has stolen.

The devil fears the truth more that he fears any other thing in the earth. This is why he has fought so hard against it since the beginning of creation. The devil knows that if he can get us to believe a lie, that we are already defeated. And, he also knows that if we ever get a hold of the truth, that he is forever defeated. This is why those who have spoken truth in Christ's Name have suffered so much – they have become a target of the one who hates all truth. Truth is the foundation upon which all apostolic ministry is built.

Apart from an understanding of truth, not what is perceived or believed, but truth as it is conceived in the mind of God, there is an absence of genuine apostolic ministry. When this happens the Church suffers because she falls into deception. Winds of doctrine begin blowing in the Church, destroying what the Spirit of Christ has created with the Church. Wolves enter in sheep's clothing, devouring the flock of God. False teachers begin teaching fallacy as fact and heresy as doctrine. When this happens, the Church is thrust into a state of apostasy.

## A Root for Apostasy in the Church

What is apostasy? It is an absence of practiced truth. Instead, tradition is setup as dogma and the result is a corrosion of the pillar of truth in the

Church. So then, apostasy happens because, in large part, there is an absence of genuine apostolic ministry in the Church. This is how vital apostles and apostolic ministry are to the Church. Without what apostles bring, we are forever doomed to repeat the mistakes of the past and become outdated and obsolescent.

Truth is timeless, opinions are but for a moment. When the Church is founded upon the truth that apostles and apostolic ministry bring, she is founded upon an eternal rock that cannot be shaken. It is this foundation that makes her what she is to society at large – a haven and place of rest from the lies of the world. Is this not what we should possess?

In business, when we become more interested in the package we present than the product we sell, our company is on the verge of bankruptcy. In the same way, when the Church loses sight of what she possesses and is called to establish in the earth under the anointing of God, she is on the verge of losing the basis for which she has been created. This is why apostles and apostolic ministry are vital to the survival of the Church, for they call her back to the center of all truth – Christ.

## The Apostolic Message

The main message of apostles and apostolic teams is Christ – they seek to glorify Him. It is this message that sets them apart from all the other ministries in the Church. Other ministries may focus our attention on truths, but in the process, we may miss the embodiment of all truth, which is Christ. Apostles on the other hand may expound upon truths, but their goal, whether realized or not, is to bring us back to the Person of truth: Christ.

It is the centrality of Christ in an apostle's mind that enables them to plug into the power of God through what can be called an apostolic faith. This faith is not a faith that can be achieved through the power of positive thinking. Rather, it is a gift from the hand of God into the heart of man. This apostolic faith is not of man, but of God, focused upon the person of Christ and centered in the words and works of Christ. Paul said, *"I determined not to know anything among you save Jesus Christ and Him crucified"* (1 Cor. 2:2).

I believe that it is important for us to know what apostles and apostolic teams will bring to the Church, so that we can receive them and receive from them all that God desires for them to bring to us. The reason why I have called attention to apostles and apostolic teams in this chapter is not to exalt them, but to enable us to receive them. For as Jesus said, *"He that receiveth whomsoever I send receiveth Me"* (Jn. 13:20a). In the same way those who reject who Christ sends are really rejecting Christ Himself.

I am not saying we should not test what someone who claims to be an apostle says. On the contrary, I am giving sound advice as to how we can tell if someone who claims to be an apostle really is one. Yet, I want us to be cognizant of this one thing: that apostles and apostolic teams have often been rejected by those to whom they were sent. It will be no different in our day.

## Apostolic Teams: The Wisdom of God

Listen to what the wisdom of God says, *"I will send them prophets and apostles, and some of them they shall slay and persecute: That the blood of all the prophets, which was shed from the foundation of the world, may be required of this generation..."* (Lk. 11:49-50). This should sober us as to the reason why God is sending apostles and apostolic teams into the earth. God is doing it, not just to bring truth to His Church, but justice and judgment to the earth in this generation.

37

God, according to His Word by which He is bound, is sending apostles and apostolic teams into the earth for a purpose, and this purpose is judgment. God uses apostles and apostolic ministry to judge between the righteous and the wicked. In the same way, as God made those who broke the law exceedingly sinful by the law, so also God uses apostles and apostolic ministry to bring forth the wickedness of the wicked to its fullness, for the purpose of executing His vengeance upon them.

So then, apostles and apostolic teams are very often God's instrument of judgment upon the world. We cannot separate this from their ministry. When we look into the lives of the apostles and apostolic teams in Scripture, this is a common theme. The ministry of apostles and apostolic teams very often brought judgment upon the ungodly. Ananias and Saphira discovered this, as did Herod and Elymas. The judgment was swift and final and the Scriptures tell us that great fear filled the Church as a result of it.

This is the heart of apostles and apostolic ministry: restoring the Church to her primary calling and mandate to be like Christ, enabling her to bring heaven on earth into the lives of those who are a part of this great Body of Believers. Because of this, there is a great responsibility resting upon the shoulders of those who are called into apostolic ministry. They have a mandate from heaven to ensure that Christ is exalted in the Church, and that anything that is not Christ-like is removed.

• Apostolic Team Ministry •

# Chapter Two

• Apostolic Team Ministry •

# Apostolic Teams Defined, and How They Work

A s you can now see, we desperately need apostolic teams in our day. Yet, for us to fully function in the realm of apostolic team ministry, we must first know what it is. This means that we need to see what the Scriptures have to say about apostolic team ministry. It is only as we understand fully the power that is released through apostolic team ministry, that we will genuinely desire it in our churches today.

The Church is called to be filled with the power of God. The power of God should not be something that we crave, but never receive. No, we are to be active recipients and receptacles of God's power. This is why Paul made it clear that His ministry was not *"in word only, but also in power, and in the Holy Ghost, and in much assurance"* (1 Thes. 1:5). This means that, without the manifest presence and power of Almighty God in our midst, we lack the assurance that His power brings.

Paul said the gospel of Christ is "the power of God unto salvation" (Rom. 1:16). He also said "the preaching of the cross is to them that perish foolishness; but unto us which are saved it is the power of God" (1 Cor. 1:18). This is what we are called to experience through the ministry of the Word of God. The Word of God is to be a source of power in the Church of God. We cannot claim to have the Word of God in us if there is not corresponding power.

One of the greatest tragedies is for those who think they know God, but know neither His Word nor His power. This is what Jesus faced when He walked the earth. There was a group of people called the Sadducees, the religious elite who didn't know the Scriptures or the power of God. Their whole lives were wasted studying something other than God's Word or power. What a tragedy to think that we know God, but deny Him with our lives!

44

Paul warned that this would be one of the prevalent signs of the last days: people who claimed to know God, but deny Him by their actions (Tit. 1:16). We cannot know God without experiencing His power. Daniel, by revelation from an angel, said *"the people that do know their God shall be strong, and do exploits"* (Dan. 11:32). There is a vital connection between knowing God and experiencing His power.

This is why I believe that understanding apostolic team ministry is so important to the Church. When the Church comes to a place of revelation of the genuine authority and anointing upon apostles, she will enter into a new era of power. God's power will be released into the Church when apostles come together in agreement and decide to work together in teams. This is one of the greatest needs in this hour – genuine team ministry.

How would we recognize team ministry? Rather than spend a great deal of time talking about team ministry, I would rather refer you to an excellent book written by Dick Iverson called *Team Ministry*. I believe that many of the questions regarding team ministry are discussed in this book. The only thing that I would like to add here is that, not only do we need team ministry in general we need apostolic team ministry, specifically.

## Defining the Apostolic Team

What is apostolic team ministry? It is two or at most three apostles working together for the purpose of establishing God's will on earth as it is in heaven. This can take the form of apostles working together in a specific territory or geographical region. Additionally, it can mean apostles partnering with one another for specific causes, ministry objects or business goals. Yet, one thing is certain about apostolic team ministry, man cannot create it.

Apostolic team ministry is divine in origin. God is the one who sovereignly places apostles together for the purpose of establishing His will on earth as it is in heaven. Apostles can be brought together by divine appointment, visions, dreams or words of prophecy. This is how God will usually work to bring apostles together into apostolic teams. In a sense, apostolic team ministry is a marriage of two distinct ministries who have a similar calling and thus are able to complement and add strength to one another.

This means that apostolic team ministry can only happen in the bond of covenant. What is covenant? Covenant is an agreement between two or more individuals. Notice covenant is not being in agreement it is an agreement. This means that those who are in covenant with one another can agree to disagree. This is what gives apostolic teams the strength necessary to stay together even when one person totally disagrees with the other or believes they have been wronged.

Covenant is what gives apostolic teams their strength. This is what enables them to survive and thrive during the times that Satan attacks them. Relationships between apostles can be preserved and strengthened when there is a covenant in place to protect the unity of the team. If, however, there is no covenant in place, the relationship will usually not be able to survive the attacks of Satan. This is why there is so much division in the Body of Christ, especially between ministers.

If we cannot agree to disagree, then we cannot remain in relationship with one another. This is what gives covenant such a power in preserving the unity of the spirit in the bond of peace. When we make covenant with another person, we are bound by our word within that covenant. If we feel wronged or slighted in the covenant relationship, we can speak our mind without giving room to the enemy to bring division in our midst.

So then, apostolic team ministry can only happen in a place of covenant where God has sovereignly joined together two or at most three apostles. When this happens, something is released into the earth called the power of agreement. It is this power of agreement about which Jesus was talking when He said *"if two of you shall agree on earth as touching any thing that they shall ask, it shall be done for them of my Father which is in heaven"* (Matt. 18:19).

When God the Father can get two apostles to come together into heart to heart agreement, there is great power and glory released into the earth. At this moment, heaven enters the earth and God's will cannot be stopped. The angels of God stand together as an army readying and waiting to enforce the decrees that are established by apostolic teams. These apostolic decrees bind the forces of hell and release the anointing of God to break the yokes of people held in captivity.

There are some strongholds that will not be broken until this level of unity enters the Church through apostolic team ministry. This is one of the reasons why I believe that the devil has, over the past two thousand years, been able to maintain his stronghold over geographic territories, such as the 10/40 window. There have not been apostolic teams in place who are ready through the decrees they establish in prayer by the Spirit of God to tear down these strongholds of Satan.

The book of acts is replete with examples of satanic strongholds being torn down. These strongholds did not come down silently. They were usually brought down through great controversy. When Paul went into Ephesus, many people heard him and believed the gospel. So great were the numbers of those who were being converted that a riot broke out between Paul and those who made statues of Diana. This was no small event, it almost cost Paul and his companions their lives.

This was the kind of power that Paul and Silas brought through their apostolic team ministry. The decrees that they prayed brought heaven's will into the earth in such a way that even the earth shook at their prayers. This is the kind of power that we need in prayer and it will only come when we have apostles who have joined themselves through covenant into apostolic teams.

## How Apostolic Teams are Established

If what I am saying about apostolic teams is true, and most of what I have said is securely founded upon the Word of God, then how can we work to see apostolic teams brought together? I believe that this is one of the most important questions that we can ask. It is crucial to our understanding of apostolic teams for us to know how they are birthed in the earth. Without this vital piece of information, any teaching on apostolic team ministry would be incomplete.

Remember, God must birth apostolic teams for them to be genuine. We cannot manufacture apostolic teams at our own whim. We can however facilitate them through a proper understanding of what God requires to bring them into being. This means we must search the Scriptures to see what they have to say about the birthing of apostolic teams. This is why I would like to see what the Scriptures have to say about birthing apostolic teams.

What do the Scriptures have to say about giving birth to apostolic teams? I believe that if we look carefully at the choosing of the twelve apostles by Jesus we will see how apostolic teams are born. There are three places where it talks about how

Jesus chose His apostles: Matthew, Mark and Luke. All of them contain different elements of what happened just prior to Jesus choosing the twelve. This is what I would like to talk about for a while.

In Mark, we see that Jesus had just completed a great healing campaign where people pressed upon Him to touch Him so that they might be healed. In Luke, we see that Jesus was under great persecution because He was doing these things on the Sabbath. In Matthew, we see Jesus having compassion upon the multitude and calling for His disciples to pray for laborers to enter the harvest. These three things are crucial in our understanding of how apostolic teams are born.

I believe that these five things must be in place for apostolic teams to be born:

1. There must be a great need that no one person alone can meet.

2. There must be something tangible preventing people from receiving the help they need from God.

3. There must be a stirring in the heart of people to pray for God's intervention.

4. We must touch the heart of God with our requests.

51

5. We may even need to spend whole nights in fasting and prayer.

Another place where we can see apostolic teams being born is in Antioch. Barnabus and Saul (Paul) had just finished ministering in Jerusalem. They must have been looking for direction from God. This is when they decided to go to Antioch to seek the will of God. Antioch must have been known as a place where people could hear from God. Notice they spent quality time with certain prophets and teachers in prayer and fasting. This is when they heard from God. *"The Holy Spirit said, 'Separate Me Barnabus and Saul* (Paul) *for the work whereunto I have called them'"* (Acts 13:2).

I believe that we can learn from this that apostolic teams do not happen by chance. They are usually brought together by God and released through the vehicle of prophecy. What we can also see is that both times apostolic teams were born, they were immediately sent out to work. This means that if we pray for God to raise up apostolic teams we must be willing to support them. This is what must have happened when Barnabus and Saul (Paul) were sent out – the Church at Antioch supported them.

## Supporting the Teams

Support is a crucial issue for apostolic teams. The Church cannot claim to have an atmosphere that is conducive to apostolic teams and yet not have a support structure in place for them. This means that we must have both sufficient prayer and financial support ready and waiting for apostolic teams before they are born. After all, how can these teams, which have a divine mandate from God, survive without the prayer and financial support of the Church?

Sometimes Believers can be so spiritual that they think that just because something is of God that it will survive even if they do not do their part. I am here to tell you that this is a false assumption. When we fail to do what God calls us to do in supporting apostolic teams, the gospel is hindered and the name of God profaned. This is why we must make a quality decision to support those apostolic teams that God raises up. Otherwise, we run the risk of not only of losing what we have been given, but also in preventing what God has desired to do in raising up apostolic teams.

One of the greatest failures of the Church is our lack of support of those who are genuinely sent by God. We ought to be ashamed of the lack of obedience in the Church today. Nearly 80% of the people who attend church do not tithe. Only 20% of the people who attend church actually tithe. Fewer still give offerings to the work of God. And we wonder why God's work is suffering and the Church is experiencing such radical moral decay. Let's get real!

Who do we think that we are fooling? God knows what He spoke to us to give. The minimum that any believer, church or ministry should give is 10% and this is pitiful when it come to Biblical standards. The Pharisees did a much better job of supporting God's work than a majority of Believers today. Think about this for a second. Think about how many times Jesus reproved the Pharisees for hindering Him and His work. Now think about what the Lord must be saying to Believers in the Church today who do not give to God's work, and then consider the fact that, at least, the Pharisees tithed.

It is so easy to be critical of others, especially those we know are doing wrong in the Word of God. It is easy to look down on the Pharisees and think: "If I had been there, I wouldn't have done that." It is easy to look at what they did to the Savior and how they plotted to kill Him, and think that was the

Pharisees – not myself. Think about this the next time you decide to hold back more from God than you know you should. The Pharisees didn't realize that their decisions were being recorded for all to see. They didn't know that they would have to stand before God and give an account for their actions. They didn't know God was watching what they were doing in secret and was judging them accordingly. Yet in spite of all this they tithed and gave to God's work. Then ask the question: "What am I doing?"

Paul said it this way, *"For we must all appear before the judgment seat of Christ"* (2 Cor. 5:10a). And again, *"the fire shall try every man's work of what sort it is"* (1 Cor. 3:13). These are the realities of God that we will all face. This is why Paul said, *"Knowing therefore the terror of the Lord we persuade men"* (2 Cor. 5:11a). If this is what Paul did in his day among people who were willing to die for their faith what do you think that he would say to us today?

I, for one, think that we need a major adjustment in our priorities, especially in the Church. When men of God have to peddle the gospel to survive, there is something wrong. When good men are corrupted by the deceitfulness of riches, and greed is applauded in the Church, there is something wrong. When Believers have to pay outrageous fees to enter the latest and greatest conference to hear from God, there is something wrong. There is sin in the house of God!

How can we tolerate something as offensive as this in the house of God? Where is the fear of the Lord, which is the beginning of wisdom? This is what we need in our day a healthy dose of godly wisdom. Not the wisdom of the world that works death, but the wisdom of God that breathes life. This is what genuine apostolic ministry is, first and foremost, the wisdom of God.

The Scripture says, *"Therefore also said the wisdom of God, I will send them prophets and apostles, and some of them they shall slay and persecute: that the blood of all the prophets, which has been shed from the foundation of the world, may be required of this generation..."* (Lk. 11:49-50). The apostolic ministry is not the wisdom of men, but of God. God is the one who has brought this ministry forth for such a time as this, to bring judgment into the house of God.

## The Apostolic Cry

I want you to understand that the apostolic ministry is being released to bring judgment, not into the Church, but also the world. Jesus said, *"For judgment I am come into this world, that they which see not might see; and they which see might be made blind"* (Jn. 9:39). This is a terrifying thought. This is not the same Jesus that most of us have heard preached by the ministers of today. The gentle Jesus of Calvary who went to the cross to slay sin has also come to judge those who desire to remain in their sin.

No wonder the apostolic ministry has brought such contention in the past. Can we expect any less in the future? The future of millions of souls hangs in the balance of genuine apostolic ministry. Will God allow these screams of desperation to be silenced by the hands of men? The Word of God will not, yes, cannot be bound. The words of apostolic ministers that are coming forth in His name will not, yea, cannot be stopped by the theologians of our day any more than they could in Jesus' day.

This is the power of apostolic teams: they bring a word that cuts to the very soul of humanity. Truly the pen is mightier than the sword. Revolutions have been sparked by the words of men. How much more then will revolutions be sparked by the Word of God? This is what we can expect from genuine apostles as they are loosed into the Church. The kingdom of heaven is about to bring a change into the earth through the release of apostolic team ministry.

This is the apostolic cry: it is a cry of one who has come forth from the wilderness wiser from the time that he has spent at the feet of God. We are talking about a man or woman who dares not consider the person of man, lest God judge him. The fear of man is the most deadly snare into which any minister can ever fall – it is a dark slippery slope leading toward hell. Those who stumble and fall into this pit rarely recover what they have lost unless they are loosed through the dynamic miracle of God.

As ministers of God and apostles of Christ, we must not stumble into this pit. We must avoid it and not pass by it; we must turn from it and pass away. Those who do not will eventually hold men up as idols, lose their faith in God and stand at the judgment seat of Christ without a prayer. Do not succumb to this deadly enemy of truth. No, choose rather to be the pillar and ground of truth. Fear Him who holds your very soul in the palm of His hand. Fear God!

The fear of the Lord is one of the overarching themes of genuine apostolic team ministry. When apostolic team ministry is functioning properly, there will be a genuine presence of the fear of the Lord. It is this fear of God that creates an atmosphere of faith in God. The air is literally charged with expectancy because people know that God is in our midst. It is this spirit of faith that gives birth to a tangible manifestation of the presence of God.

## God's Presence and Power

The tangibility of God's presence upon apostolic team ministry is what gives it its power. The power of the tangible presence of God is what makes genuine apostolic team ministry most effective. In other words, the effectiveness of apostolic teams is directly tied to the tangible manifestation of God's presence. This is why Peter and John, as well as Paul and Barnabus, had such effective team ministries. God was with them in a tangible way.

Scripture often talks about the same thing of Jesus. It will convey the idea that there were certain times when the power of the Lord was present to heal people. This means there can be in our lives different times when God is more manifest than other times. The purpose for this tangibility of God's presence is to establish us in His will – this means heaven on earth. This is God's ultimate desire for the Church to bring a tangibility of the manifest presence of God into the earth.

John G. Lake a man known as an apostle to Africa often talked about the tangibility of God's presence. There were times when Lake was so filled with the Spirit that disease would die upon touching him. The charge of God's presence in his life had subdued sickness to its proper place beneath his feet. When apostolic teams are released into the earth, there will be a charge of God's presence so strong that those churches who receive it will not be able to contain it, and hell will not be able to hold it back. As this happens, this apostolic anointing will impact the global Church and revive the work of evangelism in the world.

The force of God will be released through the lives of these men and women who are on fire with the Holy presence of Almighty God. Apostolic teams are a container for this holy presence of God. It is this unity of the spirit between the apostles in apostolic teams that releases the tangible presence of God. Talk about setting the world ablaze. Genuine apostolic team ministry releases the fire of

God into the earth for the purpose of eradicating the works of the devil.

Strongholds are torn down, devils are defeated and the world is changed. This is what apostolic teams bring to the table of Church ministry. The cup of Christ becomes evident as all partake of His glory. The flow of forgiveness in the Church is unstopped, conviction is released and bondages are broken. Apostolic team ministry releases what the devil, through our sin, has been able to hold back from us. When this happens, the treasures of darkness are released into the light and there is great rejoicing in the Church.

This is why, when we read through the Book of Acts, we cannot help but see their joy. They were joyful because they had just finished plundering hell's gates. When apostolic teams are in place in the Church and operating as they should, the gates of hell will not prevail, as Jesus said. The Church will win victory after victory after victory. We will rise up as the mighty overcomers that we were meant to be. We will be the Church triumphant, rather than a Church defeated.

An old hymn exclaims: *"Rise up, O men of God, have done with lesser things."* This is the apostolic call to the Church. When a church hears this call

61

and begins to move, hell itself trembles. Demons shake and quiver in fear when the Church comes to this place of power, for the demons know that the power of God is always greater than the power of Satan. Would to God that the Church knew the same thing, experientially, through the ministry of apostolic teams!

# Chapter Three

# Agreement in Prayer: A Team's Source of Power

*"If we would return to apostolic practice – waiting upon the Lord for apostolic power – we could then go forth to apostolic possibilities."*

*"Brethren, to our knees again, to rediscover apostolic piety and apostolic power. Away with sickly sermonizing!"*

*Leonard Ravenhill*
***Why Revival Tarries***

God, send us a Holy Ghost revival – a revival not birthed by man, a revival birthed by genuine apostolic ministry in the midst of the Church! This is the cry and longing of my heart. I long to see the works of God done in our day, as it was in the days of the apostles. I want to see the Father's will done on earth as it is in heaven. Because of this, I long to see the truths of apostolic possibility, practice, piety and power about which Leonard Ravenhill wrote revealed in today's Church. It is for this reason that this chapter is written.

I am writing to a Church that is powerless today to show the world that Jesus is the Truth, the Life and the Way. We *must* recapture apostolic power before we can truly claim to be apostles of God. And the only way that this can happen is if we rediscover the secret source of power the apostles had at their disposal – apostolic power through agreement in prayer.

There is much prayer going on in the world today. Thanks to many faithful men and women, we are seeing an awakening of prayer. This is wonderful, however, it falls far short of what the Scriptures hold as the example of prayer. The example of power in prayer in the Scriptures is unparalleled. And our meager attempts at praying fall far short of the examples posed in Scripture. This begs the question of what are we doing differently than those who found power in prayer in God's Word.

Many authors have written about various men and women of prayer in the Old Testament. I have heard how Abraham, Moses, Daniel and other Old Testament saints effectually prayed. We have also been taught some of the principles that Jesus taught the disciples when they asked Him to teach them to pray. There are many great books that touch different realms of prayer. Yet, there is one realm upon which few touch, and this is agreement in prayer.

Why is this? I believe the reason we have so little teaching on the power of agreement in prayer is that so few have experienced it. We really don't know that there is something about agreement in prayer that is different than prayer alone. Prayer done by two people in agreement is more powerful than prayer by one person alone. This is what the Word of God openly declares when it says that one can put a thousand to flight and two ten thousand (Deut. 32:30).

Jesus Himself, when talking about the topic of agreement in prayer, made this powerful statement: *"...if two of you shall agree on earth as touching any thing that they shall ask, it shall be done for them of My Father which is in heaven"* (Matt. 18:19). This is one of the most powerful prayer Scriptures ever given. Jesus here is telling us that our agreement in prayer prepares the way for His blessing like nothing else can. This is the believer's voice of victory.

It is time that we learn how to shape our world through agreement in prayer as the early apostles did. Yet, for this to happen, we must get to the place in prayer that they themselves lived; we must come to the point where we recognize our own insufficiency. As Paul said, *"Not that we are sufficient of ourselves to think any thing as of ourselves; but our sufficiency is of God..."* (2 Cor. 3:5). This is what every one of the apostles knew: they could do nothing apart from the hand of God. Can we say the same thing?

There are many in our day, especially in ministry, who cannot imagine saying such a thing. They walk around showing with shame sufficiency in themselves alone. May God help us! We must regain the humility that comes with true knowledge. We have come to say we are rich, when in reality we are poor. We think that we see, when in reality we are blind. We think we know the Word, but we have forgotten Who the Person of the Word is.

## Receiving Power From On High

Church, it is time for us to examine ourselves to see if we are in the faith presented in the Bible. This is what we are commanded to do. We need to think of ourselves soberly. We need to gain a new perspective – God's perspective. We cannot claim to have faith if we do not have the works associated with faith. Neither can we claim to be preaching the gospel if we do not have the signs of the gospel. The gospel is not in word only, but in power and much assurance according to Paul.

The gospel is the power of God. There should be power present when we preach. If there is not, then something is wrong. We need to search for a solution. We must go to the place where we want what God has for us, no matter what it will cost us. And quite honestly, pursuing God's power through agreement in prayer may cost you something. There is always a price to pay to pursue the power and will of God through united prayer. The Scriptures abound with examples of what can happen when we have agreement in prayer. They paint a clear picture of what can happen when there is agreement; yet, they also show what this agreement may cost us.

Finding the place of genuine unity in prayer does not happen overnight. It can often take years for this to happen and a quality commitment on the part of those who spend time together in prayer. We cannot expect for agreement in prayer to happen overnight. Neither can we think that just because we say that we agree that we are really in agreement. Real agreement goes beyond words to a heart level of commitment and unity. The Church has often failed to understand, realize and release the power present in the prayer of agreement. We have just not committed ourselves to one another.

The prayer of agreement of necessity involves commitment. This is why Jesus said, *"If two of YOU..."* He did not say, *"If two of anybody."* Rather (paraphrased): *"If two of you on earth who are committed likewise to My purposes and plans agree as touching anything that they shall ask, it shall be done for them of My Father Who is in heaven."* It is this place of prayer into which we have failed to enter, not because we have not known it exists, but because we have not been willing to make the sacrifices necessary to enter into it.

Most people rarely show up at group prayer meetings. Many will come for prayer teachings or even prayer evangelism, but not for prayer. For as much supposed corporate prayer that we have going on, the Church today has little personal prayer. This can be seen in pastors who spend very little actual time in prayer. Most people think that they themselves do not have time for personal prayer. This shocks and amazes me, because I cannot do without it. Prayer is my life.

Heartfelt prayer is the life force of a believer. When Believers live lives of prayer, they accomplish much for the kingdom of God. Without prayer as a vital element of our lives, we will fall far short of God's intention for our lives. This is where much of the Church is today. We are prayerless people who have fallen into the trap of seeking to substitute corporate prayer for personal prayer, and God will never allow this to happen.

The prayer of agreement is more than a corporate Church prayer meeting. The prayer of agreement is more than two people getting together to pray. The prayer of agreement is more than an evangelist praying for you and asking you if you agree with what he prayed. It is based upon a covenant commitment that you make with a person to agree with them in prayer for their lives. It is a tangible calling by God to prayer with another person.

So then, the prayer of agreement is divinely initiated. God is the one who sparks the prayer of agreement in the lives of Believers. God is the one who draws, calls and establishes the relationship between those who pray the prayer of agreement. This is the missing link between the prayer of agreement that *we* pray, and the prayer of agreement that the apostles and early disciples prayed. We must focus on this as we learn how to recover the apostolic power associated with this type of agreement in prayer.

Church, we must recognize that we have much to learn about apostolic power associated with the prayer of agreement. Because of this, we must lay aside the notion that we have all the power that the early apostles and disciples had. This is just not true. We have fallen far short of what they experienced, even among those who are famous for miracles in our midst. We just do not have the same level or latitude of power that they experienced. This is reality.

However, this does not mean that we do not have the same access to God's power that they did. No, we have the same access to God's power today as they did then. What then is the problem? Something that we are doing is short-circuiting

God's power in our lives. This means that if we can find the source of this short circuit, we can repair the problem and have access to the same power the early disciples had.

This is good news. God is no respecter of persons. He will do the same things in our day that He did in theirs if we will approach Him in the same way – through the prayer of agreement. This is why, before we go any further, I want to show you through the Scriptures that this is the pattern that Jesus set in the Church for access to power in prayer.

## Releasing Heaven on Earth

First, let us hear again what Jesus said, *"If two of you agree on earth as touching anything that they shall ask, it shall be done for them of My Father which is heaven"* (Matt. 18:19). Jesus made this statement to his apostles and disciples. This was not for everybody's ears. So then, Jesus was speaking to His disciples about how to handle disputes that came into their midst. This was how they were to handle offences. He furthermore states that when they do this, whatever they bind on earth will be bound in heaven. This is the context for what Jesus is saying.

73

The content of what He said is very clearly tying the concept of binding and loosing to the prayer of agreement. Although not the same, these two things can produce powerful results, when working together. This means that the prayer of agreement and the prayer of binding and loosing can be used by the Church to bring heaven on earth. Whatever we bind on earth through the prayer of agreement will be bound in heaven. This means that the power released through the prayer of agreement is extraordinary.

So then, in principle and practice, the prayer of agreement releases extraordinary power. When you look at the overall context for what Jesus is saying, He is really talking about how to release this power into three specific areas:

1. Being great in God's kingdom,

2. Keeping offense out of the Church,

3. Restoring those who have fallen through offense into sin and a backslidden condition.

These are the three main areas that the Scriptures reveal in this passage as to where the prayer of agreement will have an impact. A fourth would be when Jesus speaks of the prayer of agreement as the keys of God's kingdom that have power to bind on earth that which will be bound in heaven and to loose on earth that which will be loosed in heaven. Or, in other words, the prayer of agreement can have great impact in our ability to build the kingdom of God.

These are the two arenas where the prayer of agreement works in the Church and world. In the Church, it is designed to solve problems in the lives of Believers; in the world, it is designed to change history. This means, when we catch a glimpse at the awesome power that is released through the prayer of agreement, we will not only impact the Church, but the world itself will tremble at the power in our prayers. Hallelujah! We can shape our world and shake the powers that *be* so that they become the powers that *were*. Praise God!

Church, we have an awesome source of power at our disposal to solve our problems. Men of God, we have an awesome tool in our hands that we can use to literally change our world, Church and ministry. Once you get a hold of it, the prayer of agreement will radically change your life, Church ministry and world. This is what God designed it to do.

The prayer of agreement is powerful, and I believe it is the source of power revealed in the apostolic teams shown in Scripture. An example of this is Peter and John when they were going to the temple to pray, as was their custom. Here is God painting for us a picture of what they were doing to make this miracle that Peter was about to do happen, and He says they were going to pray as was their custom. In other words, they were used to praying for one another and with each other.

## Opening the Door to Unity

Look at what happened after Peter healed the lame man. Suddenly, all Jerusalem hears news of what Peter and John had just done. Then, they were thrown in jail, beaten and released. They were told not to preach the gospel anymore. Then, the Scripture says, *"They lifted up their voice with one accord..."* (Acts 4:24). They prayed, and when they prayed, *"...the place was shaken where they were assembled together..."* (v. 31) This is the power of apostolic teams: they open the door to unity in the Church.

It was Peter and John's prayer time, praying the prayer of agreement as an apostolic team, that opened the door for them to be able to work the will of God in the Church on earth. The prayers that they were praying as a team were producing powerful results. God was causing His will to be done on earth as it is in heaven. This is what prepared the way for an unprecedented revival among the Jewish people, and opened the door for God's glory, miracles and more in the Church. This is the pattern of Scripture.

Another apostolic team was Barnabus and Paul, who received their commission into apostolic ministry through the vehicle of prayer. It is evident from the passage in Acts 13 that Paul and Barnabus were used to spending time together in prayer. From this, it is easy to believe that they knew how to pray the prayer of agreement. And we can also easily believe that they prayed regularly with and for one another.

What happened after Paul and Barnabus spent time in prayer with one another, praying the prayer of agreement? Immediately, you see God open the door for them to speak the Word of God to the synagogues in Salamis (Acts 13:5). Not only that, but Paul and Barnabus were ready for a power encounter with Elymas, the sorcerer in Paphos (v. 8). Needless to say, they won this power encounter through the power of God – power that, I believe, was released through the prayer of agreement that they had prayed as an apostolic team.

This is the kind of power that we need in the Church today. This is why I want you to understand that this power is available to us through the vehicle of team ministry. As a team we can accomplish more than we can alone. This is why I believe that apostolic teams are vital to the advancement of God's kingdom. I am persuaded through my study of Scripture that God has designated apostles to work together within the framework of apostolic teams.

Because of this, it is easy to see why God must divinely arrange specific apostolic teams. As an apostolic team, those involved in the team will be apostles. They will have a similar calling and complementary gifting. In certain cases, apostolic teams can be a husband and wife, as in the case of Andronicus and Junia (Rom. 16:7). This is usually the exception rather than the rule for apostolic teams. Yet, apostolic teams always exist on the basis of covenant.

Covenant is the foundation upon which apostolic teams are built. Neither apostle within an apostolic team can accomplish what God has called them to do alone; they need each other's help. Because of this, they will have to learn how to relate to one another, work with one another and pray with one

78

another. This is how the unity of the Spirit is established within apostolic teams, and this is where division can often creep into it.

Many hardships can be avoided within apostolic teams if we develop realistic expectations of the team member or members. As I said previously, apostolic teams are usually made up of two and at most three apostles. When we develop realistic expectations, God will enable us to avoid the pitfalls of pride, arrogance and misunderstanding that can often drive a wedge between apostolic teams. This is why we need to learn how to cultivate humility of heart as apostolic team members.

An apostolic team is made up of two different people with complementary strengths. Therefore, we must understand our strengths and weaknesses as well as our team members' strengths and weaknesses. If we learn about the person with whom we are called to work in ministry, it will help us greatly in uniting with them through the vehicle of the prayer of agreement. And it is this vehicle of the prayer of agreement that will give an apostolic team its power with God and man.

God wants us to have this power, and He has provided every vehicle for us to walk in it. The only thing left up to us is: Will we do His will? This is the question we face as apostles and apostolic teams: Will we do the will of our Father in heaven? This can be an easy question if we have already allowed our hearts to be sold out to the Father. And this is what we must do to see the power of God released through the prayer of agreement in apostolic teams.

# Chapter Four

# Receiving Revelation of Apostolic Team Ministry

**B**elieve it or not, I did not receive this revelation of apostolic team ministry until I had actually started experiencing the fruits of it. I had enjoyed the blessing of being in an apostolic team without even realizing it. God was doing things in my life that I had prayed would happen for years, and yet, until I was sovereignly joined together with another man in prayer, it didn't happen. In other words, understanding this revelation has made an enormous difference in my life, and it will yours too.

Because of this, I am excited about sharing with you how I received what God gave to me in this book. This revelation is not a new revelation, in that, it is clearly revealed in Scripture in the lives of the early apostles. Additionally, many ministers whom we might think of as apostles or at least great evangelists functioned according to this pattern of apostolic team ministry. Jesus Himself is the one who instituted this style of ministry in the Church. We would do well to follow His example.

## Where Today's Church Is Going

Why has the Church, then, lost this idea of apostolic team ministry? I believe that one of the main reasons that we have not clearly understood apostolic team ministry, as presented in Scripture, is because the ministry model that we have used consists of an independent western worldview. The ministry models that most seminaries and Bible schools use is incomplete and doesn't contain a frame of reference for ministries that function outside of the local church.

Peter Wagner, one of the foremost leaders amidst the New Apostolic Reformation, calls this difference one of Sodality vs. Modality. In his excellent commentary on the Book of Acts, he outlines the differences between Sodality and Modality leaders and their leadership styles. According to Wagner, Modality-style leaders have the spiritual gifts necessary to function well at a local church level. This is the style of ministry that we have used to train seminary and Bible School students.

This, I believe, is the reason why we do not have an overall understanding of apostolic team ministry: we have had no frame of reference for their existence. Because of this, we are seeking to work out the details of how exactly apostolic ministry should function in the Church. As such, I hope that you will see this book on apostolic team ministry as a work in progress. The truth is we are learning what apostolic ministry is and how it should function in the Church.

The Church itself is changing with the release of the revelation of apostolic ministry. As a result, many top leaders in Christendom are trying to hear what God is saying and see what He is doing. There is a general consensus amongst leaders that a transformation in the Church is coming, yet, most who are saying this recognize that what they see, they see *through a glass darkly.*" I believe that this fundamental change in the Church is ushering in an apostolic Church. This will be the subject of my next book.

So then, this message on apostolic team ministry is vital to understanding the practical day-to-day workings of apostolic ministries. What I am seeking to do is lay a Biblical foundation for how apostolic ministries should function within the Church. This is why I am seeking to show how apostles and apostolic ministries functioned in teams rather than as individuals. I want a solid foundation to be laid for how apostles should function in the Church today.

I am persuaded that this message is extremely important to the health of the apostolic movement arising in the Church. Without the balance and accountability that team ministry brings, there is a good chance that this movement will derail itself. The concepts and principles being presented are so new that there is great potential for abuse to enter the Church and cause us to lose touch with the will of God as revealed in Scripture. If this happens, we run the risk of ruining many lives and causing many to fall. God does not want this to happen.

This is why I ask that you hear the wisdom that the Lord has given to me regarding apostolic team ministry. I do not claim to have a full understanding of apostolic teams – only a sufficient revelation of the Scriptures that reveals the concepts thereof. God has given me both experiential and doctrinal understanding of the revelation of apostolic team ministry. I have tasted of the good fruits of apostolic team ministry, and this is what I am seeking to convey to you, the reader.

## Where We Began

As I said in the beginning, this revelation of apostolic team ministry came as a result of a regular prayer meeting. God sovereignly joined together another man and myself to pray for one another. We did this week after week, experiencing radical changes in our lives through the miracle of answered prayer. For him, God's blessing came upon his career, marriage, family and home. For me the blessing was evident in ministry, business and my personal walk with the Lord. I cannot convey to you how extraordinary the things that happened were or how evident God's blessing was upon us.

This caused me to do a lot of soul searching. I spent a great deal of time asking myself why we were seeing such great results. I myself had spent a great deal of time in prayer for many years without ever coming to the place of fruitfulness that I was now experiencing. I had been to many prayer meetings with many different individuals, yet, never with the results that I was now experiencing. I knew that there was something different, but I didn't know what it was until God began to reveal it to me.

When we first started this prayer meeting, it was based upon James 5:16a, which says, *"Confess your faults one to another, and pray for one another, that ye may be healed."* So, week after week, this is what we began to do. We confessed our faults to one another and prayed for one another. We have done this for the past 3 years. During this time, God regularly caused miracle after miracle and blessing upon blessing, all in response to fervent prayer.

Probably the most visible sign of God's blessing was the increase in our income. Financially, we just started taking off. This other man's salary has doubled for the past three years, and he is now in a position to move even further in business. To date, I have had several articles that I have written appear in national magazines. Additionally, I have started a graphic design business with no prior background as a graphic artist and have created ads that are now appearing in national magazines like *Entrepreneur*. And this is just a small sampling of what God has done in our lives over the past three years.

I have discovered that it is God's will for me to be blessed. God wants you and me to live and walk in His blessings. We are to experience the abundant life that Jesus promised. This is why I want to encourage you to hear what I am saying regarding apostolic team ministry. I believe that, as God's apostles begin to function in accordance with the principles set forth in this book, that there will be a release of God's blessing upon the Church like we have never seen.

God is ready, willing and waiting to do exactly this for you and me. God was actually waiting upon me for years to get me in a position to receive this revelation of apostolic team ministry. This is why God poured His blessing upon our prayer meeting. He was seeking to teach me the things that I am now teaching you. I learned that true prayer must have at its center a willingness, not only to receive from God, but also to confess its need to Him. This is what happened as we committed ourselves to James 5:16. God taught us the fundamentals of prayer.

## Receiving God's Greater Blessings

As we progressed in prayer, we entered into deeper and deeper levels of the blessing of God. There was a specific point in the prayer meeting where the Lord showed me that we were moving from James 5:16 (confession, mutual prayer and healing) to Matthew 18:19 (the prayer of agreement). It was then that I believe we started moving into apostolic team ministry. The strength of our prayers went to a new level, and we saw a greater blessing and provision released into our lives. It was then that I knew that we had touched upon something, and that God was seeking to teach me something.

As a result, I started seeing the parallel between apostolic team ministry and the prayer of agreement outlined in Matthew 18:19. I could see that this Scripture was specifically suited for apostles working together as a team. When Jesus made this statement, He was in fact speaking to His apostles and disciples. This is when I began to see how foundational this understanding of agreement in prayer was for apostolic team ministry to function. Apostolic teams achieve their greatest effectiveness through prayer.

This is the pattern laid out in Scripture. From Peter and John, to Paul and Barnabus, to Paul and Silas, the common theme is that of apostolic teams. Jesus sent out His apostles as teams in the Gospels. The Early Church sent out its apostles this way all through the Book of Acts. Paul the apostle functioned this way in ministry throughout his entire life. Apostolic team ministry was a commonly held belief in the Early Church, and those who have done great things in the Church have largely operated this way.

Why then have we so little teaching on apostolic teams? I believe that we have operated under the assumption that all effective ministry proceeds from the local church, and this is simply not true. According to Peter Wagner, missiologically, most of the Church-related growth has happened through Para church organizations rather than local churches. This means that our underlying assumption of effective ministry has been wrong, and as a result, our foundation for effectiveness has been erroneous.

In order for us to have a Biblical foundation for effective ministry, especially as apostles, we must identify how genuine apostolic ministry looked and how it functioned in the Church in the New

91

Testament. Once we have begun to grasp how apostles functioned in the New Testament, then we must move forward into effective apostolic ministry. This is why I have written this book to identify how apostolic ministry functioned within the Church in the New Testament. I have proven through the Scriptures that apostles functioned as teams in ministry. This, then, is how apostolic ministry should function today.

# Chapter Five

# Transferring the World's Wealth to the Church

O ne of the key themes that many leaders in the Body of Christ are talking about today is the great transfer of wealth that will pass from the world to the Church. According to many leaders, God is getting ready for a supernatural outpouring of wealth into His Church. This supernatural transfer of wealth will release the finances necessary to complete the evangelization of the world as Jesus foretold in the Gospels when he said, *"This gospel of the kingdom will be preached in all the world"* (Matt. 24:14).

As you may have noticed on the cover of this book, I have chosen to use an ATM machine to signify Apostolic Team Ministry. I want you to gain an understanding of the importance of the apostolic mantle to releasing the wealth of the world to the Church. Additionally, I want you to see that our source for blessing is not of this world, although we live in this world. God alone is the source of supply for His Church – this will never change.

The Church today is about to get plugged into something so amazing through the ministry of apostolic teams, that we are going to see the greatest transfer of wealth to the Church. We are going to literally see heaven manifest itself on earth. Our prayer for the kingdom of God to come and for the will of God to be done will be answered by God Himself, as apostolic teams begin to pray. This release of apostolic prayer will usher in the wealth of the wicked to the Church and the wealth of God to the world.

Get ready! We haven't seen anything yet! The time has come for the Church to enter into a new day of leadership in the world. No longer will we take a backseat to the world; we are going to tell the world to move over, because we are taking over the driver's seat. Hallelujah! This is what we are going to do through the ministry of apostles and apostolic teams. The power of God will be so evident that fear will fall upon those who oppose us.

## The Third Day Church

The fear of God is about to enter into the Church. This holy reverential fear of the Lord will burn away our ulterior motives and agendas. No longer will we seek our own, as Paul said everyone around him was doing, but rather we will seek the things that are of Christ Jesus. We will no longer "play Church" – we will *be* the Church. The ashes that we have heaped upon ourselves will be shaken off, and the holy robes of righteousness placed upon us. We will wear the garments of praise and prayer as a Church ready to meet her beloved Bridegroom, Christ Jesus.

Hear me! The day of the old is passed away. The funeral dirge has driven this style of ministry to the burial place and there is a dawning of a new day. This new day is complete with a new style of leader and ministry within the Church. The Church is shifting gears from first to second to third. We are entering the third day of the Church, and because of this we are entering a new season of beginnings. The old has passed away and the new has come.

Within this new day is a new way. The way things have worked in the past will no longer work. We cannot claim that yesterday's manna will satisfy the multitudes. They are searching for new manna bread from heaven that will satisfy their souls. This hunger will be quenched and filled by a new order of minister, an apostolic one, and by a new order of Church, an apostolic one. This is why apostolic team ministry is so vitally important: it will prepare us for the greatest transfer of wealth the world has ever known by showing us a Jesus Whom we have never seen before.

We are about to see Jesus in a different way than we have seen Him previously. We have seen Jesus as the Prophet, Pastor, Teacher and Evangelist, but we have yet to see Him as the Apostle. Because of this, we may not recognize Him as the Apostle. Our hearts may burn within us as we are conversing with Him, as did the hearts of those on the road to Emmaus, yet we may not immediately recognize Him. This is why we must be careful not to reject Him, as He appears to us as the Apostle through the ministry of apostles.

## The Apostolic Revolution

Much of the teaching that we have on the apostle right now is in seed form. We really don't know how apostles look. This is why we must remain open in our hearts to the seed of the Word of God regarding apostolic ministry. There must be a willingness in us to receive what the Lord reveals, even if it doesn't look like the seed that was sown. The seed that is sown never looks like the plant that is born. According to Scripture, God gives it a different body.

The body of information that will come forth on the apostolic ministry is years away. Within this time period, many will claim to be apostles who are not. There will be rumors of apostolic ministry that are not true. We will see the seed of apostolic ministry, but not the body of it. This is why we must be careful not to reject the voice of the Lord to us in the process of the restoration of the apostolic ministry. We must allow our ears to be attuned to God's voice – one ear listening to Scripture, the other ear listening for the Rhema Word of God.

I believe that as we do this, and as the ministry of apostles comes forth, an avenue will be created for the greatest transfer of wealth that the world has ever known. This is why team ministry will become so important to the Church. Without this team concept of ministry, we will have no genuine accountability. This is one of the main reasons why God is bringing apostles forth as teams; we need one another to hold each other accountable.

The Body of Christ has sorely been broken because of the lack of accountability among her leaders. The real sin in Christian leadership today is that no one is willing to submit to the other in love. We cannot hear one another over the pride that is in our own hearts. This is why so many leaders refuse to fellowship with one another; they cannot stand to humble themselves in the sight of the Lord that He might lift them up. I believe that the greatest sin in Christian leadership today is pride.

America's leaders have a wall of pride that we have so eloquently puffed up through our inflated sense of self-importance. We guise our pride with words of faith in hopes that no one will see what is really in our hearts. We allow the fallacy to continue that we are special in the eyes of God and somehow exempt from His dealings. We sin in public through our private lives that are drenched with the sin soaked sheets of lust from a sex-crazed world.

We lust for power, we lust for wealth and we lust for fame. Our sex-crazed culture has spawned in us the sin of lust. We cannot stop ourselves from our covetous ways. We covet earnestly the best gifts, but the way of love, we have not known. Our services are filled with a clanging gong and tinkling symbol. The sound of the spirit of the world fills the Church. This is what we have come to know as acceptable in the Church, and this is why there is so little conviction of sin or discipline for sin in the Church.

The spirit of holiness demands that we allow God to remove from us the excrement of the world's system from our lives. We cannot approach a holy God and hold onto our sin. We must let go of our sin or we will let go of God. This means that leaders in America must let go of pride, otherwise we will be destroyed by the sin of pride. There can be no middle ground on this issue. We will either let go of our pride or we will lose the anointing of God.

I don't know about you, but the prayer of my heart is the prayer of David: *"...take not Thy Holy Spirit from me"* (Ps. 51:11). I repent for my pride, dear Jesus. Forgive me for how I have offended you with the pride in my heart. Until we as ministers are able to come to this place of repentance for the pride in our hearts, we are on the verge of missing the greatest move of God's Spirit in the history of the world. We will not be able to see or receive the apostolic ministry that God is birthing in our day.

## The Apostolic Way To Wealth

Which will you choose? Will you choose the highway of the upright or the low way of the wicked? The choice is ours. We can change. If we are willing to take the baby steps that God is asking us to take to repent of our pride, then He will turn those baby steps into gigantic feats of faith. The mountains that have held us back from fulfilling the will of God will be turned into dust before our feet, because we will have learned the secret of possessing the world – meekness.

Jesus said, *"Blessed are the meek: for they shall inherit the earth"* (Matt. 5:5). This is one of the most mocked statements in Scripture. Many have mocked the meekness and gentleness of Christ. Yet, believe me that now is the time when meekness will not be seen as weakness. Those who are meek will truly start to possess all things through the ministry of apostles and apostolic teams. Why?

Because, one of the chief characteristics of apostolic ministry is meekness.

Listen to what Paul said about himself to the believers in Corinth, *Now I Paul myself beseech you by the meekness and gentleness of Christ..." * (2 Cor. 10:1a). Paul was willing to humble himself and debase himself so that Christ might be exalted. This was the life of the great apostle Paul, one of humility, meekness and gentleness. God allowed many things to happen in Paul's ministry for the purpose of rooting out pride in his heart.

Listen to what God allowed to happen to Paul, *"And lest I should be exalted above measure through the abundance of revelations, there was given to me a thorn in the flesh, the messenger of Satan to buffet me, lest I should be exalted above measure"* (2 Cor. 12:7). Many people have wrestled with the question of what this thorn in Paul's flesh might have been, but few have examined what it did to his spirit – it humbled him. God humbled him, lest he should be exalted above measure. These things were the dealings of God with Paul the apostle.

If God allowed these things to happen to Paul the apostle, do you think that He will exempt us from these types of thorny situations, which are designed to humble us? I think not! Paul realized that in him dwelled no good thing. He, in and of himself, was not sufficient for the task that God gave to him. This is why he rejoiced in his own weakness and failings in the sight of God. Paul knew that his weakness could be turned into Christ's strength, if he allowed Jesus' grace to work in him.

We need to hear this message in our day. We need to remember that our salvation is only by God's grace; *"...it is the gift of God: not of works, lest any man should boast"* (Eph. 2:8-9). This means that we didn't earn our place into heaven. Christ didn't give us our position in His kingdom because of our worldly status and position. No. He chose us because we were weak in what He called us to do. Our weakness is what makes His grace in our lives even grander.

Grace is what makes the difference in the Church. Without this key ingredient in our lives, everything that we do is stained by pride. As such any transfer of wealth into the Church will not come the world's way through works, rather, it will come God's way by grace. This means we need to expect God to give us what we do not deserve, rather than what we do deserve. This is what grace is all about: it is receiving what you could never achieve by yourself.

This is God's way. It is the apostolic way. It is the way of Christ. And it is the way of the cross. As the old hymn says, *"At the cross, at the cross where I first saw the light, and the burden of my heart rolled away; it was there by faith I received my sight, and now I am happy all the day."* This is something that I believe we need to understand in our day – the way of the cross is the way of Christ. And this way, the way of the cross is the only way that wealth of the world will ever be transferred into the Church.

Listen Church, God will never allow us to be polluted with the unsanctified wealth of the world. This is why the work of the cross is vital to the transfer of wealth into the Church. Without the work of the cross, the wealth of the world cannot be sanctified for the use of the Church. The cross is the altar of the Church; it is this altar that sanctifies the gifts given in the Church. Without this understanding of the altar of the Church, we cannot receive the wealth of the world into the Church.

## Sanctifying The Offering

I believe that we have lost sight of this truth in today's Church. Somehow we have forgotten what Jesus said to the Pharisees regarding their giving and how they thought more of the gift than the things that made the gift holy.

Listen to the words of Jesus to the Pharisees:

*"Woe unto you, ye blind guides, which say, whosoever shall swear by the temple, it is nothing; but whosoever shall swear by the gold of the temple, he is a debtor! Ye fools and blind: for whether is greater, the gold, or the temple that sanctifieth the gold? And whosoever shall swear by the altar, it is nothing; but whosoever sweareth by the gift that is upon the altar, he is guilty. Ye fools and blind: for whether is greater, the gift, or the altar that sanctifieth the gift?"* (Matt. 23:16-19).

These are strong words and serious charges from the Savior. Jesus had an issue with the Pharisees regarding their teaching about giving. They made the gift more important than the altar and the gold more important than the temple. Their focus was wrong, and as a result they lost something more valuable than the gift or the gold;

they lost the sanctification that came with the altar and the temple. Could this be one of the reasons why there is such an absence of morality in the Church today?

I think we need to recapture the truth that the altar and temple sanctify what we give. What does this mean to us as New Testament Believers? It means that we need the cross and Church to sanctify the gifts that we give to God. Without this sanctification of the gifts that we give, they are unclean things in the house of God. And, whenever we place mere gifts and monetary gain from man higher than the cross of Christ or the Church of God, we have committed serious sins in the sight of God.

So then, we need to examine ourselves to see if there is any wicked way of handling wealth in us. Do we think more of our money than the Church? Is our job more important to us than the Church? Are we willing to lay our lives down to protect our wealth, and yet, not bear the reproach of the cross of Christ? Where have we put our faith – in what we possess or in the timeless treasures of eternity? These are serious issues to God and things to which we will be held accountable as Believers in Christ.

Am I saying money is bad? No, not at all. I believe that money, when it has been sanctified to holy purposes through the cross of Christ and the Church of God, can be a blessed gift from God. This is the transfer of wealth that many, including myself, have been saying will pass from the world to the Church. This is why we need a fresh understanding of the work of the cross and Church in our day. We need apostolic revelation regarding how the Church, in conjunction with the cross of Christ, sanctifies the gifts we give to the Church. We need fresh manna revelation of the cup of blessing that Christ has deposited in His Church.

It is this revelation of the cup of blessing held within the communion of Christ that will release to the Church an unprecedented level of sanctification, especially in the area of giving. When this happens, the gifts given will be holy, not because of their size or amount, but because they have been given in accordance with the command of God. It is this release of sanctification upon the gifts given by the Church and to the Church that will release tremendous wealth into the Church. This is a holy thing.

For such a long time, we have treated the offering of Christ with disdain. The world has despised it, because men of God have misused it to heap up wealth for themselves. And no matter how we justify it, it is still wrong in the sight of God. This is why there must be change. We must allow Christ to confront and challenge our beliefs about giving. Things that have been entrenched in the Church for generations must change if we are to receive from God that which He desires to give. Unless this happens, there will not be sufficient sanctification of the gifts we give to meet heaven's standards in order to affect a transfer of wealth from the world to the Church.

Do you see how serious this matter is to God? We have glossed over the importance of allowing God to sanctify our gifts through the cross and Church. We have forgotten the challenge of Scripture that, just because we give to God, it does not necessarily mean that He is going to receive it. Cain murdered Abel over this very thing. Hear the word of the Lord to Cain after he gave his offering: *"Why are thou wroth? And why is thy countenance fallen? If thou doest well, shalt thou not be accepted? And if thou doest not well, sin lieth at the door"* (Gen. 4:6-7).

Church, this sin is lying at the door of the Church because we have not treated the offering of

Christ as a holy thing. Because we have despised the offering of Christ and have not given as we should or in the way we should, many of our gifts to God have not been accepted. This means that we must repent for our false attitudes regarding giving, and be restored to the truths contained in the Word of God regarding giving, that it is a holy thing in the sight of God.

## Fulfilling Our Destiny

The release of apostles and apostolic ministry will do this in the Church. It will create an atmosphere of holiness in regards to the offering of Christ. The Church will be restored to her first love in the area of giving, and the charlatans will be exposed in the sight of all. God will not tolerate those who use His Name to fleece His flock. This is a word of warning to ministers to examine themselves, lest they be found in error and judged accordingly.

We must judge ourselves, lest we fall under the judgment of God. Do not think that just because we are living in New Testament times, that God will not judge our sins, especially in regards to the offering. Throughout Scripture, God has judged those who defiled the offering, whether in the Old or New

Testament. From Cain to Eli's sons to the Pharisees to Ananias and Saphira, all who sinned in this area were judged harshly and without remedy by the hand of God.

This is the truth, even though it may be hard to hear. Whether the offering is defiled from the pulpit or pew, it will be dealt with severely by God. God will not allow us to taint His offering by our sin even for the sake of a good cause. Neither will He receive what we give if it is not in accordance with His Word. This is one of the main reasons why so many have given to churches/ministries, and yet have not received from God. They have not given according to the Word of God. How we give is just as important, if not more important to God, than what we give. Yet, this doesn't mean what we give is unimportant.

Giving is important to God, the Church, ministers, Believers and the world itself. Apostles and apostolic teams will bring an increased recognition of the importance of sanctified giving. When giving is done in accordance with the Word of God, it releases tremendous blessing. Sanctified giving is the instrument that God will use to release the wealth of the world to the Church. Apostles and apostolic teams release the grace necessary to walk in this realm of giving consistently.

Grace is the essence of all true apostolic ministry. Apostles and apostolic teams walk in a realm of grace few of us understand. The grace they possess enables them to lay aside earthly possessions for the sake of the kingdom of Christ. As such, God gives them more, for they have been willing to give their all to Him for the purpose of furthering His kingdom on earth as it is in heaven. Through their sacrifice of all, they gain all they need and more is supplied to them, and those who help them in their apostolic work. This is the realm of the hundredfold blessing spoken of by Christ.

The hundredfold blessing is an apostolic blessing that is released to those who have been willing to sacrifice everything in support of the mission of Christ in the earth. When Believers are willing to do this for the sake of Christ's Kingdom, the Kingdom then begins to draw near to them. Remember, it is the Father's good pleasure to give us the Kingdom. He is only waiting for a people who are willing to lay aside everything they have to receive all that He has.

Apostles and apostolic teams have the ability to enable the Church to live in this realm of sacrificial giving, such that, the doorway to heaven's blessings are opened. Sacrificial living opens the floodgates of heaven, such that a tidal wave of blessing is released to the church in the form of answered prayer. When our prayers are answered, good fruit is born, and the kingdom of heaven prevails. As the kingdom of heaven prevails on earth, the treasures in darkness are taken as spoils of war.

As the old adage states, *"To the victor goes the spoils."* When the Church begins winning the spiritual conflict she is facing by walking in the realm of genuine apostolic team ministry, tremendous wealth will be released to the church from the world through the power of answered prayer. Answered prayer will pave the way for the victory of the church. The victory of the Church will remove every obstacle preventing the evangelization of the world. The current financial barriers preventing the expansion of the kingdom will fall through the release of sanctified giving, sacrificial living and genuine apostolic team ministry. Then, as Jesus said, *"the end shall come."*

• Apostolic Team Ministry •

## *Other Books Available from Lighthouse Publications*

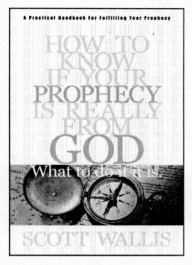

### How to Know if Your Prophecy is Really from God

One of the most important books on prophecy available for Believers. If you have ever received a prophetic word, then this book will help you discern if that word was from God, and if it was, what to do with it to see if fulfilled.

Author: Scott Wallis
Retail Price: $11.99
ISBN: 1931232415

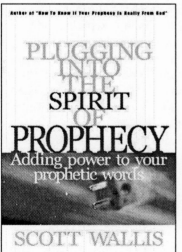

### Plugging into the Spirit of Prophecy

God has designed every believer to walk in the prophetic. You can learn how to flow in the Holy Spirit of prophecy. This exciting book will teach you how to do this and more. You will experience God's awesome power through the prophetic word.

Author: Scott Wallis
Retail Price: $11.99
ISBN: 1931232210

## Decade of Destiny

A powerful prophetic word detailing what God is doing in our days. First written in 1991, this timeless book has proven to be an accurate window into the future. Discover what God is saying to His Church today!

Author: Scott Wallis
Retail Price: $11.99
ISBN: 0964221195

## Understanding the Ways of God

You can understand the mysteries behind God's ways. No longer wonder why God does what He does – you can know. As you read this exciting book, you will learn secret after secret of walking in the ways of God. Unlock the potential God has placed inside of you as you learn the ways of God!

Authors: Ken & Pat Kucera
Retail Price: $11.99
ISBN: 0964221152

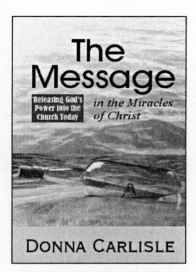

## The Message in the Miracles of Christ

Recently, researchers have discovered that there may be hidden coded messages in the actual text of the Bible. Could it be that the miracles of Jesus also reveal hidden messages of what God is doing in our day? Discover the answer as you read this exciting book!

Author: Donna Carlisle
Retail Price: $14.99
ISBN: 0964221136

## The Third Reformation is Coming

Prophetic leaders have been declaring for several years that a third reformational movement of the Holy Spirit was about to begin. Find out what this third reformation is and how it will radically change the Church and your life.

Author: Scott Wallis
Retail Price: $9.99
ISBN: 0964221144

**Growing in the Spirit**

Taking from life examples, Pastor/Prophet Rudy Clark reveals principles of spiritual growth. Through many life lessons, God has taught Reverend Clark the values and virtues that have made him the man he is today. Experience freedom as you learn how to reach your fullest potential.

Author: Rudy Clark
Retail Price: $14.99
ISBN: 0964221160

**These and other Christian books from Lighthouse Publications are available at participating local Christian bookstores, Amazon.com & Bn.com.**

**To order books directly from Scott Wallis:
Visit www.ScottWallis.org**

## Ministry Headquarters
2028 Larkin Avenue
Elgin, IL 60123
(847) 468-8139

# • Additional Resources •

# • Additional Resources •

• Apostolic Team Ministry •